W9-CCT-692

ROYAL CHILDHOOD

ROYAL CHILDHOOD

ANNA REYNOLDS • LUCY PETER

ROYAL COLLECTION TRUST

CONTENTS

BUCKINGHAM PALACE
FAMILY HOME

One of the most instantly recognisable buildings in the world, Buckingham Palace has come to symbolise the British monarchy itself. The Palace is the setting for The Queen's official work in receiving visitors, heads of state, prime ministers, guests attending garden parties, and those receiving honours. The great many works of art which have been collected and commissioned by successive monarchs over the last 500 years provide a magnificent backdrop to all these events. Buckingham Palace also houses the staff who serve The Queen in her role as Head of State of the United Kingdom and Head of the Commonwealth, and the offices and apartments of ladies-in-waiting, private secretaries and housekeeping staff.

Given the very public and official character of the building, it is easy to forget that Buckingham Palace is also a family home, and has been since George III first purchased Buckingham House in 1762. The newly wed and newly crowned King wrote to his Prime Minister, Lord Bute, that he considered the new house 'not meant for a Palace but a retreat'. Situated in a relatively rural location across the royal park, it was still close to St James's Palace, the centre of official court life and the location for the formal and public court functions which played such an important part in eighteenth century society.

Buckingham House was intended to provide a comfortable, more sheltered, and domestic environment for George III and his wife, Queen Charlotte. Fourteen of the royal couple's fifteen children were born there. The eldest six

OPPOSITE:
Johann Zoffany,
*George, Prince of Wales, and
Frederick, later Duke of York,
at Buckingham House*, 1765
RCIN 404709
•

are represented with their parents in three unusual porcelain figure groups
(shown above), produced by the Derby porcelain factory and based on a group
portrait by Johan Zoffany which dates from 1770. The two eldest brothers link
arms affectionately whilst echoing the formal, adult stance of their father. The
two-year-old Prince Edward plays with a dog while the youngest child, Princess
Augusta, sits on her mother's lap.

One visitor to Buckingham House in 1802 commented, 'Here are the
comforts of a family home, with the grandeur and some of the ornaments of
a palace'. Several paintings by Zoffany emphasise this family atmosphere and
the informality of children within the palatial surroundings. The painting on

ABOVE:
Derby porcelain,
*George III, Queen Charlotte and
their six eldest children*, 1773
RCIN 37020–2

•

OPPOSITE:
Allan Ramsay,
George III (1738–1820),
*c.*1761–2
RCIN 405307

•

ABOVE LEFT:
John Singleton Copley,
*The Three Youngest Daughters
of George III*, 1785
RCIN 401405

•

ABOVE RIGHT:
Franz Xaver Winterhalter,
The Royal Family in 1846.
The painting shows Queen
Victoria and Prince Albert with
five of their nine children
RCIN 405413

•

page 6 shows George, Prince of Wales, and Frederick, later Duke of York, in Queen Charlotte's drawing room on the first floor of Buckingham House, now part of the Picture Gallery. The boys, who are aged two and one, have not yet been 'breeched' into adult clothes but instead wear coats, and are shown beneath portraits of their parents. Sir Anthony Van Dyck's *Three Eldest Children of Charles I* hanging above the fireplace emphasises the dynastic connections between the ruling House of Hanover and the Stuarts a century earlier.

A sense of natural childhood exuberance and sisterly affection is captured in John Singleton Copley's image of the three youngest daughters of George III and Queen Charlotte (above left). Dated 1785, it shows the two-year-old Princess Amelia sitting in a carriage, holding the hand of her sister, the eight-year-old Princess Sophia and looking towards Princess Mary, aged nine, who plays a tambourine. These are the very same children who were believed to have played with the doll's house, shown opposite, between 1780 and 1790, and

Details of the dolls' house belonging to the daughters of George III, 1780s

probably even to have made some of the furnishings themselves. According to tradition this 'baby house', as it would then have been known, was made by a carpenter on the Royal Yacht for the young princesses. Evidently a toy that was much played with and enjoyed, it is both a rare survival and an important illustration of late Georgian tastes in interior design.

The next monarch to embrace and expand the potential of Buckingham Palace as a family home was Queen Victoria. She took up residence at the age of 18, on 13 July 1837, soon after acceding to the throne, and over the next 20 years her marriage to Prince Albert resulted in the birth of nine children. All of them were born at Buckingham Palace except their second son Alfred, who arrived during the summer months at Windsor Castle. In a departure from royal protocol, Prince Albert attended the births of all nine of his children.

The royal couple quickly realised that their London home was inadequate for the needs of their growing young family. During the Queen's first pregnancy

ABOVE LEFT:
Dean and Co., *The Royal Children
in the Nursery*, 1845
RCIN 605924

•

ABOVE RIGHT:
An invoice for bottles of honey water,
ivory toothbrushes, a satinwood
hairbrush and cold cream bought
from Gattie & Peirce of 57 New Bond
Street for the Royal Nursery in July and
August 1846. Similar invoices list toys,
books and clothing purchased for
the Queen's children.

•

OPPOSITE:
Eugène Louis Lami,
*The Grand Staircase at Buckingham
Palace, State Ball, 5 July 1848*
RCIN 919902

•

a nursery had been hurriedly created from a breakfast room in the north wing – remote from the rest of the royal living quarters. A more satisfactory solution was created by the architect Edward Blore. By enclosing the east side of the courtyard with a fourth wing, enough space was created to contain nurseries and additional bedrooms.

The value that Queen Victoria and Prince Albert placed on their family led them to rearrange the pictures in several of the rooms as dynastic portrait galleries, emphasising the familial blood line to the English throne and the connections between the various courts of Europe. One which still remains in place today is the set of late Georgian portraits of Queen Victoria's parents, grandparents, uncles, aunt and cousin by artists including Sir William Beechey and Sir Thomas Lawrence. These were hung around the Grand Staircase and the arrangement is recorded in a watercolour by Eugène Louis Lami of 1848 (opposite).

Princess Elizabeth, later Queen Elizabeth II, was known as 'Lilibet' by her family and grew up very close to her parents, the Duke and Duchess of York,

ABOVE LEFT:
The Duchess of York with Princess
Elizabeth and Princess Margaret
outside 145 Piccadilly, 1930
RCIN 2112011

•

ABOVE RIGHT:
Princess Elizabeth and Princess Margaret
standing outside Royal Lodge, 1934
RCIN 2112504

•

OPPOSITE:
Princess Elizabeth's first radio broadcast
was made during a 'Children's Hour'
programme from Windsor Castle,
12 October 1940
RCIN 2002152

•

and sister, Princess Margaret Rose, who was four years younger. The family of four lived a quiet, happy life split between a townhouse, 145 Piccadilly in London, and Royal Lodge in Windsor Great Park, which had been taken on as their country home and renovated when Princess Elizabeth was six years old (above right). During the first year of her life the princess spent a significant proportion of time living with her grandmother, Queen Mary, at Buckingham Palace, while her parents were on an extended tour overseas.

With the death of King George V in 1936 and the abdication in the same year of her uncle, King Edward VIII, Princess Elizabeth moved into Buckingham Palace with her parents, now King George VI and Queen Elizabeth. The two princesses spent most of the war years living at Windsor Castle where they had been moved for their safety. The whole family returned to Buckingham Palace after the war. After her marriage to Prince Philip, Princess Elizabeth lived for a short time at Clarence House, and then following her accession,

Princess Elizabeth
and Princess Margaret at
Buckingham Palace, c.1940
RCIN 2002174

•

OPPOSITE:
The Queen, The Duke of
Edinburgh, Prince Charles and
Princess Anne in Buckingham
Palace garden, photographed by
Lord Snowdon in 1957
RCIN 2808695

•

as Queen in 1952, the royal couple moved into Buckingham Palace to raise their family there (opposite). Until they went away to school The Queen's children generally spent weekdays at Buckingham Palace in London, weekends at Windsor Castle, Christmas at Sandringham, Easter at Windsor and the summer at Balmoral Castle in Aberdeenshire – a pattern that still largely remains today.

BIRTH AND BIRTHDAYS

Princess Elizabeth of York was born on 21 April 1926 at 17 Bruton Street, the London home of her maternal grandparents, the Earl and Countess of Strathmore. A sister, Margaret Rose, was born in August 1930 at Glamis Castle in Scotland when Princess Elizabeth was four years old. She was nicknamed 'Bud' by her older sibling. It had long been the custom at a royal birth for Privy Counsellors and ladies-in-waiting to be present as witnesses in an adjoining room. However, since 1894 only the Home Secretary was summoned to attend. Thus Sir William Joynson-Hicks was present at The Queen's birth and J.R. Clynes arrived soon after the birth of Princess Margaret. In 1948 it was announced that, as the attendance of a minister of the Crown at a birth in the Royal Family was neither a statutory requirement nor a constitutional necessity, the practice would be discontinued.

To commemorate the birth of each daughter, their mother, the Duchess of York commissioned china tea sets from the Paragon China Company. The service made for Princess Elizabeth is decorated with pairs of magpies and is known as the 'Two for Joy' pattern (shown right), while that made for Princess Margaret Rose has two brightly coloured birds, alongside marguerite and rose flowers to symbolise her names.

Crowds gathered outside Buckingham Palace on 14 November 1948 to celebrate the birth of a son to the

OPPOSITE:
Crowds gathered outside Buckingham Palace to celebrate the birth of Prince Charles in 1948
RCIN 2814255
•

BELOW:
Paragon China, 'Two for Joy' tea service, 1927
RCIN 19085
•

The Duke and Duchess of
Cambridge leaving St Mary's
Hospital with their newborn son,
Prince George of Cambridge,
Tuesday, 23 July 2013

22-year-old Princess Elizabeth (shown on page 18). Both Prince Charles and Princess Anne (b.1950) spent their first years living at Clarence House, but moved into Buckingham Palace upon the death of King George VI. Prince Andrew (b.1960) was the first child born to a reigning monarch since Princess Beatrice, born to Queen Victoria over 100 years earlier. Both Prince Andrew and Prince Edward (b.1964) were born in the Belgian Suite, a room on the ground floor of the west-facing garden front, which is now used to house visiting heads of state.

In 1982 Prince William was the first heir presumptive not to be born in a royal residence. Instead he was delivered at St Mary's Hospital Paddington, as was his brother Prince Henry (soon known as Harry) two years later, and his own son, Prince George in 2013. Both Peter and Zara Phillips had been born in the same hospital. Princes William and Harry would grow up at Kensington Palace. Their cousins Princess Beatrice and Princess Eugenie, daughters of the

Duke of York and Sarah, Duchess of York, were born at the Portland Hospital and spent much of their childhood at Sunninghill Park in Berkshire.

The birth of a new royal baby is a cause for celebration for both the family itself and the wider population, symbolising the continuity and history of the royal family, as well as hope for the future. The official announcement of a birth in the direct line of succession is displayed in the forecourt of Buckingham Palace for the large crowds who have gathered to await news. In the case of Prince George of Cambridge (b.2013), the announcement, signed by the senior medical staff, was set on an easel (above left). The notice of the birth of Prince Charles in 1948 was attached to the railings. Royal births are usually celebrated with a 21-gun salute. Letters of congratulation and gifts are received from all over the world, as well as from close friends and family.

ABOVE LEFT:
The official bulletin on the forecourt of Buckingham Palace announcing the birth of the son of The Duke and Duchess of Cambridge on Monday 22 July 2013
RCIN 6877

•

ABOVE RIGHT:
Illuminated congratulatory Resolution from the Lord Mayor and the City of London Corporation to commemorate the birth of Prince George, 2013

•

BELOW:
Gold locket belonging to
Princess Victoria, 1820
RCIN 65295

As for all children, birthdays provide an opportunity for presenting gifts to the royal child. Some are simple and sentimental, others on a much grander scale. For her first birthday, Princess Victoria received a gold, heart-shaped locket containing a lock of hair from each of her parents and engraved with their interlinked initials, 'E' and 'V'. The inscription around the edge of the heart reads 'Present from her Mother to her beloved Victoria on the First Anniversary of her Birthday 24 May 1820' (left). Sixty-three years later Queen Victoria made a blanket for her most recent granddaughter, Princess Alice, of pink and white wool, with a silk lining. It is embroidered with the cypher of Queen Victoria and the date, 1883 (below left).

On her fourth birthday Princess Elizabeth was given a Shetland pony, which she called Peggy, by her grandfather, King George V (opposite). She took riding lessons with the groom, Mr Owen, in Windsor Great Park surrounding Royal Lodge, and was able to ride on her own by the age of six. This was the start of a love of horses which remains to this day. One of Peggy's horseshoes was carefully preserved and hammered to the cupboard door at Royal Lodge (shown on page 45), alongside those of other important equine family members.

LEFT:
Blanket made by Queen Victoria
in 1883 of wool with silk lining

RIGHT:
Alpaca baby blanket given to
Prince George by the President
of the United States and
Mrs Obama, 2013

Princess Elizabeth and Princess Margaret with Mr Owen and 'Peggy', Prince Elizabeth's first pony
RCIN 2108324

Birthdays also present an opportunity for a more public type of birthday present to a royal child. For her sixth birthday in 1932 Princess Elizabeth was given a miniature thatched cottage, 'Y Bwthyn Bach', or The Little House, by the people of Wales (shown overleaf). This came complete with electric lighting and running water as well as cutlery, utensils and furniture. At 22 feet wide and 15 feet high, it was built to two-fifths scale and contained a living room, kitchen, bedroom and bathroom. Princess Elizabeth and Princess Margaret looked after it themselves and for many years it was their favourite toy. It was installed in the grounds of Royal Lodge, where it still remains in regular use by the current generation of royal children. One of the photographs on page 25 shows Princess Elizabeth and her mother the Duchess of York climbing a ladder leaning against the cottage during the thatching of the roof.

OPPOSITE:
The Welsh Cottage in 2014
•
RIGHT:
Princess Elizabeth outside the Welsh
Cottage, *Y Bwthyn Bach*, 1932
RCIN 2112192
•
BELOW RIGHT:
Princess Elizabeth
and the Duchess of York
at the Welsh Cottage, 1932
RCIN 2112199
•

Prince Charles and
Princess Anne in the Picture
Gallery, Buckingham Palace,
photographed by Lord Snowdon
in November 1956
RCIN 2814387

Princess Elizabeth
riding with her father
King George VI and sister
Princess Margaret, 21 April 1939
RCIN 2002139

•

A birthday is also an occasion for an official portrait commission. To satisfy public demand, photographs are often released to the press to mark the occasion. The photograph on the previous page shows Prince Charles and Princess Anne in the Picture Gallery at Buckingham Palace, one of a series of photographs taken by Lord Snowdon to mark the eighth birthday of the Prince. A photograph of Princess Elizabeth riding in Windsor Great Park with her father and sister was taken on her thirteenth birthday and released by Central Press Photographs Ltd (left).

Over the years Buckingham Palace has been the venue for many children's birthday parties. The celebration of Prince Leopold's sixth birthday is depicted in Eugenio Agneni's watercolour of 1859 (opposite, left). It shows the young guests dancing in brightly coloured fancy dress outfits, against the equally colourful decorations of the Ball Supper Room. Queen Victoria wrote of the occasion, 'It was really a very pretty Fête, & the Children all enjoyed it so much, no one more, than little Leopold.'

Children's parties were still being held at Buckingham Palace for The Queen's children in the twentieth century. Sixteen children attended Prince

Edward's fifth birthday party in 1969, enjoying crumpets with honey, Twiglets, egg sandwiches and sausages on sticks. Tea was in the Old Schoolroom on the east front and the children watched the new film *Chitty Chitty Bang Bang*. Sometimes at these parties a conjuror would perform or the children would swim in the Buckingham Palace pool. Birthday cakes were an important part of the celebration – for Prince Charles's fourth birthday he was presented with a cake in the shape of an elaborate galleon. Children's parties were also held to celebrate fireworks night, accompanied by jacket potatoes cooked in foil on the bonfire and eaten from paper plates. Christmas parties were usually held in the Bow Room and The Queen would distribute gifts to each of the children from the Christmas tree positioned outside.

ABOVE LEFT:
Eugenio Agneni,
*The Children's Fancy Ball
at Buckingham Palace*,
7 April 1859
RCIN 919909

•

ABOVE RIGHT:
Birthday cake in the shape of a
galleon made for Prince Charles
on the occasion of his fourth
birthday, 14 November 1952

•

CHRISTENING

The christening of a royal child is an occasion of both personal religious significance for the family and symbolic importance for the country since, as 'Defender of the Faith and Supreme Governor of the Church of England', the monarch has a very close connection with the church.

Baptism is the formal welcome of the new baby into the Church of England and the ceremony is bound up with tradition and history. Today, these are usually small private daytime occasions, with formal photographs released after the event, although in the eighteenth and nineteenth centuries a royal christening was often a much more formal and public occasion, with the celebrations continuing until late into the evening. The banquet held in 1853 to celebrate the christening of Queen Victoria's ninth and final child, Prince Leopold, is illustrated overleaf. The enormous four-tier christening cake in the centre of the table was described in *The Times*: 'the base being decorated with wreaths of white and red roses. The two upper divisions were faced with crimson satin, on which were displayed, in white letters, the initials P.L., surmounted by a crown varied with ornaments of pearls and white roses. The cake was crowned with a golden cup, filled with flowers. Oval ornaments, representing the four seasons, were placed round the cake.'

Royal christenings are usually held within a royal residence, although one exception to this was the baptism of Princess Eugenie in 1990, which was held at a public Sunday morning service in the chuch of St Mary Magdalene in Sandringham. Royal godparents are known as 'sponsors' and the baby is baptised with holy water from the river Jordan. The Archbishop of Canterbury

OPPOSITE:
Prince Charles in his christening gown on his mother's lap. King George VI, Queen Elizabeth and The Duke of Edinburgh are also present, 15 December 1948
RCIN 2814350

Louis Haghe, The christening banquet for Prince Leopold in the Picture Gallery of Buckingham Palace, 28 June 1853
RCIN 919917

•

often conducts the ceremony, as in the case of the baptism of Prince George in 2013. The hymns for his christening were *Be thou my vision* and *Breathe on me, Breath of God* with processional organ music by J.S. Bach.

The Lily Font (opposite, right) was commissioned by Queen Victoria in 1840 for the christening of her first child, Princess Victoria, which was held the following year on the Queen and Prince Albert's first wedding anniversary. The font has been used for all royal christenings since then except for that of Princess Eugenie. Made of silver-gilt, the font takes the form of a central flower surrounded by a border of water-lilies and leaves, the lilies being a traditional representation of purity and a symbol associated with the Virgin Mary.

Queen Victoria also commissioned a set of christening robes made of white silk-satin with Honiton lace overlay (shown on page 34). Designed by Janet Sutherland, 'Embroiderer to The Queen', they were conceived to resemble the dress worn at Queen Victoria's wedding one year earlier and have been worn by

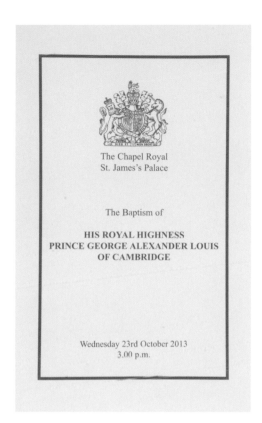

over 60 royal babies since then. Due to the fragility of the robes, now over 170 years old, in 2008 The Queen commissioned a replica from her Dresser, Angela Kelly, which was first used for the christening of James, Viscount Severn, son of the Earl and Countess of Wessex. Most recently, the robes were worn by Prince George in 2013, shown on page 35.

Three of The Queen's children were christened in the Music Room at Buckingham Palace – Prince Charles in 1948, Princess Anne in 1950 and Prince Andrew in 1960. So too was Prince William, whose christening in 1982 is recorded in a watercolour by John Ward (page 36, top). As the central room on

ABOVE LEFT:
Order of Service for the baptism of Prince George, 23 October 2013

•

ABOVE RIGHT:
Barnard & Co.,
The Lily Font, 1840
RCIN 31741

•

the first floor of the west wing, its curved windows over-look the garden. The high domed ceiling and blue scagliola columns lend a suitably ecclesiastical feel. Other royal children have been christened in the private chapels at Windsor Castle, Buckingham Palace and St James's Palace, as well as St George's Chapel, Windsor. For children baptised in the Music Room at Buckingham Palace, formal photographs are taken in the White Drawing Room following the service. By tradition these show the various generations of the family together with the child's sponsors seated on and around the yellow silk-covered sofa, the newly christened child in the centre (page 36, bottom).

OPPOSITE:
Sir George Hayter,
The Christening of The Prince of Wales,
25 January 1842 (detail), 1842–5
RCIN 403501
•

RIGHT:
The Duchess of Cambridge carries her
son Prince George after his christening
at the Chapel Royal in St James's
Palace, 23 October 2013
•

LEFT:
Rotating carousel from Prince
Charles's christening cake,
15 December 1948
RCIN 48958

•

RIGHT:
Prince Edward's
Christening cake,
2 May 1964

•

Christening cakes, cut after the ceremony and distributed to guests, are an important part of the celebration. The cakes for Queen Victoria's children were made by Mr Mawditt, Her Majesty's Confectioner and the Queen kept samples in small silver boxes. The christening cake for a first born child traditionally incorporates the top tier of the parents' wedding cake. This was the case for the principal cake made for Prince Charles and also for his son, Prince William. Two other cakes were also made for the christening of Prince Charles and put on display in the White Drawing Room after the ceremony. One of these was topped with a silver carousel made by wounded ex-servicemen, which is engraved with the arms of his mother on one side, and of his father on the other (above left). The baby in a cradle is rocked by the lion and unicorn from the Royal Arms. Prince Edward's christening cake was decorated with intricate

OPPOSITE, TOP:
John Ward, *The Christening of
Prince William in the Music Room
at Buckingham Palace*, 1982
RCIN 453064

•

OPPOSITE, BOTTOM:
Diana, Princess of Wales, holding
Prince William and surrounded by
other members of the Royal Family
in the White Drawing Room,
4 August 1982

•

Franz Xaver Winterhalter,
The First of May 1851
RCIN 406995

royal icing, decorated with an 'E' and topped with a baby in a silver cradle (shown on page 37, top right).

For her christening on 29 May 1926, Princess Elizabeth was presented with a silver cup and cover by her godfather and great, great uncle, Arthur, Duke of Connaught (shown opposite, top left). In the painting shown above, the infant Prince Arthur can be seen receiving a gift from his own godfather, the Duke of Wellington, in a portrait by Winterhalter. *The First of May 1851*, commemorates the first birthday of the infant Prince, the eighty-second birthday of the Duke of Wellington, and the opening day of the Great Exhibition, visible in the distance. A letter from Queen Victoria to her son, who at the age of 21 enquired

what had happened to the jewel casket represented in the painting, reveals that in fact it was an invention of the artist and that the Duke's gift had in fact been a gold cup and toys.

In 1948 Queen Mary gave Prince Charles a silver gilt cup and cover (above centre). This gift had a poignant significance – as Queen Mary wrote in her diary, 'I gave the baby a silver-gilt cup & cover which George III had given to a godson in 1780 – so that I gave a present from my g[reat] grandfather, to my great grandson 168 years later'.

Continuing in this tradition, in 2013 the Royal Navy presented the Duke and Duchess of Cambridge with a silver cup to mark the baptism of Prince George (above right). This cup bears the name of HMS *Prince George*, the Royal Navy battleship which was launched in 1895 and was named after the future King George V. It is engraved with the date 1898, when it was presented to the ship and its recent presentation connects two royal children born six generations apart.

ABOVE LEFT:
Christening cup and cover given to Princess Elizabeth by the Duke of Connaught in 1926–7
RCIN 50931

•

ABOVE CENTRE:
Cup and cover given to Prince Charles by Queen Mary in 1948. It was originally made in 1762–3.
RCIN 49950

•

ABOVE RIGHT:
Cup and cover, given to Prince George of Cambridge in 2013. It was originally made in 1898.

•

GROWING

The royal family has always kept careful records of their children's growth and development. A series of baby books, compiled by royal parents provide detailed accounts of certain milestones such as first words, favourite bathtime toys and general likes and dislikes. Princess Elizabeth's early months were carefully captured in her Progress Book (below). The first page notes the details of her birth, as well as the names of her parents and grandparents, while later pages record her monthly weight and nature – during her early months she was described as 'active', 'very healthy', 'vigorous' and 'contented'. Her first visit to Buckingham Palace Garden was recorded as occurring on 14 May 1926.

A century earlier, samples of Princess Victoria's hair were carefully collected and arranged into a series of albums by her mother, the Duchess of Kent. Each lock was tied with a pink ribbon and slips of paper, attached under each piece of hair, record the date and place where the sample was taken (shown right).

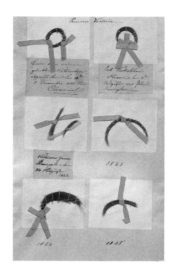

RIGHT:
Princess Elizabeth's
Progress Book, 1926

•

OPPOSITE:
Casket containing
the first teeth of Queen
Victoria's children, c.1860
RCIN 52617

•

ABOVE:
Page containing samples of
Princess Victoria's hair taken
from an album compiled by
The Duchess of Kent, 1820–5
RCIN 1006154

•

My dul Dec: 1847.

Princesses Helena and Alice and Prince Alfred drawn by their mother, Queen Victoria, in 1847
RCIN 980122

•

Like her mother, Queen Victoria enjoyed collecting personal objects designed to capture the fleeting likenesses of her children as they grew. The first teeth of Queen Victoria's five eldest children are preserved in a blue glass casket, decorated with the Queen's monogram (shown on page 40). Each child was allocated a separate compartment, arranged in two layers, and each tooth was wrapped and labelled in a series of small paper envelopes.

An accomplished artist, Queen Victoria also produced a large number of drawings, paintings and etchings of her children. One example, dated 1847,

shows Helena, Alfred and Alice playing with a toy horse on wheels (opposite), very like those owned by Princess Elizabeth in the 1930s. Queen Victoria frequently recorded her growing children's accomplishments in her journal. On 16 January 1844, for example, the Queen wrote, on returning to Windsor Castle from Claremont, how they 'found Alice in great force, so lively, & she can crawl a little now,' while, 'Vicky remained downstairs the greater part of the evening, & was full of fun & mischief.'

Queen Victoria, like many parents, was anxious to keep permanent records of her children's appearance. She commissioned 14 marble carvings of their arms, legs and feet. One example, attributed to Mary Thornycroft, shows Prince Alfred's left arm when he was seven months old (above). In order to overcome the difficulties inherent in capturing a likeness from a baby that does not keep still, a plaster cast was taken while the child was sleeping, and then worked up in marble by the artist at a later date. The Queen was particularly fond of these sculptures and they were displayed throughout her lifetime in the private apartments at Buckingham Palace.

Marble carving of Prince Alfred's left arm, attributed to Mary Thornycroft, 1845
RCIN 34581

ABOVE LEFT:
Blue quilted shoes
worn by Albert Edward
(later Edward VII), 1842
RCIN 52392

•

ABOVE CENTRE:
Silk baby shoes worn by
Prince Edward (later
Edward VIII), 1894
RCIN 71936

•

ABOVE RIGHT:
First pair of booties worn
by Prince George
(later George V), 1865
RCIN 71921

•

Royal parents also liked to preserve their children's footwear. An inscription on the sole of a tiny pair of shoes belonging to Prince Albert Edward, later Edward VII, tells us that they had been worn in July 1842 when the prince was only eight months old (above left). The shoes are made of blue velvet with a button tie to secure them at the ankle. Similarly, a pair of quilted silk satin slippers, belonging to the future King Edward VIII, were lovingly preserved by his parents King George V and Queen Mary (above centre). The slippers have been skilfully hand-decorated with small, metallic crowns.

A customised toy cupboard door provides one of the most personal examples of the royal family keeping an informal record of their children as they grew and is reminiscent of the markings on walls and door frames found in many homes (opposite, left). Originally part of a cupboard in the nursery at Royal Lodge, the door was subsequently moved to Clarence House. Pencil lines, primarily along the right-hand side of the door, indicate the rising heights of the royal children. Horseshoes have been pinned to the central panel in memory of

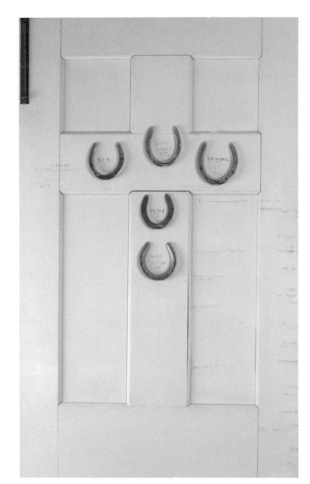

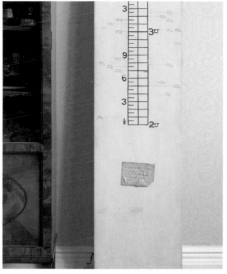

LEFT:
Door from nursery cupboard at
Royal Lodge containing height
marks and horseshoes
RCIN 8890553

•

ABOVE:
Height chart for the children of King
George V and Queen Mary, c.1894–1910
RCIN 54554

•

Princess Elizabeth's first ponies. Two lines, both dated 13 June 1936, indicate that Princess Elizabeth was almost a foot taller than her younger sister at the time these heights were taken. The heights of the six children of King George V and Queen Mary are similarly recorded on a chart, now housed at Frogmore. The bottom-most line of the chart records the height of the Duke and Duchess's youngest son, Prince John.

CARING

A young infant needs continual loving care to ensure he or she is kept fed, warm, clean and well rested. Traditionally monarchs have shared the care of their children with one or more nurses or nannies, and many royal children have formed close and long-lasting relationships with those who have provided invaluable support to their mother and father. As the centuries have progressed royal parents have tended to be more directly involved in caring for their child on a day to day basis, although some assistance is still the norm. Queen Victoria's daughter Princess Victoria is shown affectionately being dried by her nurse after taking her evening bath in an intimate engraving created by her mother (page 49, top left).

The nanny's domain was the nursery, a room or set of rooms, and her responsibilities included caring for the children in numerous ways – feeding them, helping them sleep, dressing them and bathing them. Usually they had the assistance of a nursery maid and a nursery footman who would bring the children's food each day, clean and service the pram and so on. The nanny or nursery maid slept either with the child in their bedroom, or in an adjoining room. They travelled with the family, providing a sense of stability during the children's formative years and setting out rules and discipline, and instilling good manners into their young charges.

OPPOSITE:
Princess Elizabeth with the infant Prince Charles, photographed by Cecil Beaton on 14 December 1948
RCIN 2999884

•

BELOW:
Silk and lace-trimmed bassinette, c.1930. Queen Elizabeth's children slept in a bassinette until they were old enough for a larger cot.

•

LEFT:
Princess Elizabeth,
photographed by Marcus Adams
on 3 March 1927
RCIN 2943708

•

RIGHT:
Letter from nanny
Clara Knight, 'Allah', to the
Duchess of York, 8 March 1927
RCIN 2943709

•

BUCKINGHAM PALACE

If mummy looks into my wide open mouth with a little magnifying glass she will see my two teeth —

Elizabeth ; quite well & happy !

allah.

Mrs Clara Knight was nanny to Princess Elizabeth and Princess Margaret, but had also been nanny to their mother as a child (opposite, right). Affectionately known as 'Allah' to the children, a childish contraction of Clara, she stayed with the two princesses from their birth until her death in 1946. Working with her was a young Scottish nursery maid, Margaret MacDonald (known as 'Bobo') who remained close to The Queen for more than 60 years. Her sister Ruby MacDonald played a similar role for Princess Margaret. When Princess Elizabeth's parents set off on a six-month tour of Australia when she was eight months old it was Allah who sent photographs of her progress to the Duke and Duchess of York, accompanying one with a letter saying 'If Mummy looks into my wide open mouth with a little magnifying glass, she will see my two teeth' (shown above). Allah looked after the children in the nursery at

145 Piccadilly, which was on the top floor with windows overlooking Green Park, and in the nursery at Royal Lodge.

Nurse Helen Lightbody had initially worked for The Queen's uncle, the Duke of Gloucester, as nanny to his two sons, Princes William and Richard before taking up the position of nanny for Prince Charles in 1948 when he was only a month old. She was known to Prince Charles as 'Nana'. Working with her was Mabel Anderson as nursery maid, who would later become nanny to Prince Andrew and Prince Edward, and came out of retirement to play the same role for Peter Phillips (shown on page 51). When Mabel was nanny she was assisted by June Waller.

The Buckingham Palace nursery used by the children of The Queen and Prince Philip was situated at the corner of the east front on the second floor,

ABOVE LEFT:
Etching by Queen Victoria of Princess Victoria and her nurse, 9 April 1843
RCIN 506836.by
•

ABOVE RIGHT:
Princess Elizabeth and Princess Margaret with their nanny, Clara Knight, 1931
RCIN 2112057
•

ABOVE LEFT:
Sir Edwin Landseer,
Princess Alice asleep, 1843
RCIN 403097

•

ABOVE RIGHT:
Princess Alice's carved and
gilt wood cradle
RCIN 1453

•

BELOW:
Hot water can and baby bath decorated
with sprays of yellow roses
RCIN 55920–1

•

overlooking the Mall and Constitution Hill. This bright, cheerful room has large windows and adjacent bedrooms for the children and nursery staff. It served as the children's playroom and contained cupboards with books and toys, as well as a comfortable sofa and open fire, in front of which clothes and cloth nappies were dried on the fender. The nursery was also where the children ate their meals at a large, round table and the adjoining bathroom was the location for their evening bath. The children would visit their parents each morning during the week when they were in London and their parents would also often visit in the early evening to join in bathtime or to read books at bedtime. In the corridor outside, overlooking the lift shaft was a large photograph of Prince Charles and Princess Anne looking at a globe and silhouetted

Prince Charles and Prince Richard, son
of the Duke and Duchess of Gloucester,
with nannies Ellen Woodburn, left, and
Mabel Anderson, 3 May 1951

OPPOSITE:
Prince Charles and Princess Anne
photographed by Lord Snowdon
in November 1956
RCIN 2937630

•

LEFT:
Pram used by Prince Andrew
and Prince Edward
RCIN 98602

•

RIGHT:
Forward-facing pram used
by Prince Charles
RCIN 98601

•

against a pale background, which was taken by Lord Snowdon (opposite).

Until they were old enough to have a governess, who took responsibility for them during school hours, it was traditional for the nanny and her nurse maids to look after the royal children during the daytime as well as having responsibility for helping them sleep at night. They would take their charges out in the pram in the nearby royal parks, and would settle them down for a nap outside in the garden weather permitting. One pram, shown above left, was made by Millson's, and was used for Prince Andrew and Prince Edward. When Prince Charles was able to sit in a more upright position his flat pram was swapped for a forward-facing version (above right), which allowed him to enjoy the world around him.

RIGHT:
The Prince of Wales on an outing
in St James's Park, with
nanny Mabel Anderson,
14 November 1950

•

RIGHT:
Etching by Queen Victoria of
the Princess Royal with
her nurse, 1841
RCIN 816581
•

BELOW:
Silver feeding cup, 1865
RCIN 46811
•

BELOW:
Silver breakfast set given
to Prince George of
Cambridge, 2013
•

Feeding is of paramount importance for any growing young child. Another etching by Queen Victoria shows Princess Victoria at the age of nine months in the arms of her nurse, being fed from a bottle (above right). At Christmas in 1865 a small silver feeding cup was given to the six-month-old Prince George (later King George V), designed to provide the young child with milk before he was able to consume solids (above left). Silver items associated with feeding and engraved with personal inscriptions remain popular gifts for royal babies today. In 2013 Prince George of Cambridge received a silver breakfast set from Mr Joseph Muscat, Prime Minister of Malta, which consisted of a spoon, plate, cup and egg cup (shown left).

High-chair in birch
with a cane seat and cushion
RCIN 33185

Nurseries often contain miniature furniture designed to suit the scale of its small inhabitants. One beautifully made royal example of such furniture is a chair constructed from birch-wood, with a caned back and seat (above). A bar across the front stops its occupant from falling down and it can be screwed to a base to raise it to the height of a standard table. A high-chair is a necessity for the messy business of feeding a young child who is just starting to learn about the tastes and textures of different foods. A photograph dating from 1896 shows two of Queen Victoria's great grandchildren. Prince Albert (later George VI), evidently not yet able to support himself sitting upright, is strapped into his high-chair and stares at his older brother Edward with great interest (overleaf). The comfortable and upholstered small red chair shown on page 57 was used by Princess Elizabeth as a child.

Prince Edward and Prince
Albert of York, June 1896
RCIN 2373307

LEFT:
Princess Elizabeth's red chair
·

BELOW:
Nursery chairs belonging to
Prince William and Prince Harry,
Princess Beatrice and Princess
Eugenie
·

LEARNING

Historically, royal children were educated at home. From the age of five, the young Princess Victoria had a governess, Louise Lehzen (right), who was responsible for her overall education. Growing up at Kensington Palace during the 1820s her principal master was Dr George Davys, although she had separate tutors for French, writing, geography and arithmetic. For handwriting practice she repeated sentences within pencil ruled diagonal lines. One of her marbled paper-covered exercise books shows that by the age of only eight she had developed a beautiful style of writing (below left). Careful records were kept of the hours and subjects for these lessons as well as the princess's behaviour, which ranged from 'very good' to 'rather impertinent' and 'very naughty'.

   Similar books record the daily schoolwork of later royal children during the nineteenth century. Queen Victoria chose John Neale Dalton as tutor for her grandsons, Prince Albert Victor and Prince George (later King George V), and he taught them for 14 years, firstly at Windsor Castle and then onboard the

ABOVE:
Carl Friedrich Koepke, *Louise, Baroness Lehzen*, c.1842
RCIN 420414
•

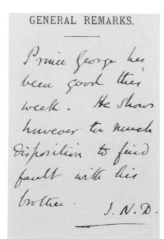

OPPOSITE:
Spelling game belonging to Princess Elizabeth
•

LEFT:
Sample of Queen Victoria's handwriting, aged eight
•

RIGHT:
Page from the daily record of Prince George (later King George V), dated Saturday, 23 September 1876
•

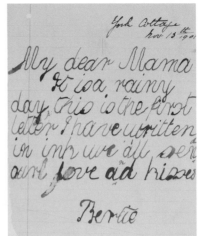

ABOVE LEFT:
Sydney Prior Hall,
*Prince Albert Victor and
Prince George of Wales*, 1876
RCIN 920780
•

ABOVE RIGHT:
First letter in ink written by
Prince Albert Frederick (later
King George VI), 1901
•

cadet training ship HMS *Britannia*, which Prince George joined at the age of 12. Dalton's record of Prince George's work for the week of 23 September 1876, notes that the 11-year-old prince was taught for 22 hours in the subjects of religion, music, arithmetic, geography, writing, Latin, French and English. In most cases the tutor's remarks were good, although on one occasion he writes that Prince George shows 'too much disposition to find fault with his brother' (page 59, bottom right). A more co-operative vision of brotherhood

Letter written by
Prince Albert Frederick
(later King George VI) to his
parents at the age of six, 1901
•

is shown in the watercolour by Sydney Prior Hall, where the two princes are seen crossing the River Dee on the cable bridge at Abergeldie in the same year (opposite, top left).

Letters in the Royal Archives reveal the progress of royal children in learning to write. A charming letter from 'Bertie' – Prince Albert Frederick, later King George VI – to his parents dates from 1901 when the young prince was only six years old. He writes, 'My darling mama & papa. We hope you are quite well and not seasick. Did you have a big wave when you went through the Bay of Biscay? We send you love and a lot of kisses. From your loving Bertie'. The note is finished with a number of kisses and a drawing of a little person, perhaps the young letter writer himself (shown opposite). A letter from later the same year proudly notes that 'this is the first letter I have written in ink' (opposite, top right).

Princess Elizabeth was also educated at home, firstly at 145 Piccadilly, then later with Princess Margaret in a newly created schoolroom at Buckingham Palace. The schoolroom was built on the second floor of the north wing looking out over Constitution Hill, with lessons sometimes held outside in the summer-house. Their governess was Marion Crawford (shown above), nicknamed

Princess Elizabeth and Princess Margaret outside Royal Lodge with their governess, Marion Crawford, 1934
RCIN 2112483

ABOVE:
French word games belonging to
Princess Elizabeth, *c*.1935

•

BELOW:
The Happy Farm, written by
Princess Elizabeth, 1934

•

'Crawfie', who taught Princess Elizabeth from the age of five and stayed with the family for 16 years. School hours were regular, with a timetable that included arithmetic, grammar, literature and history in the mornings. Queen Mary took a particular interest in the education of her granddaughters, making suggestions to the governess on lessons, and taking the children on educational visits to museums. History was a favourite subject for Princess Elizabeth, and she also excelled at French which she had learnt from infancy and spoke with an excellent accent. The princess was set examination papers which were blindly marked. Later she was also taught constitutional history twice a week by Sir Henry Marten, Vice-Provost of Eton College.

At the age of eight, Princess Elizabeth wrote a charming short story called *The Happy Farm*, shown left. Dedicated 'To Sonia, My dear little friend and lover of horses', it was evidently never given to the intended recipient – perhaps because it appears to

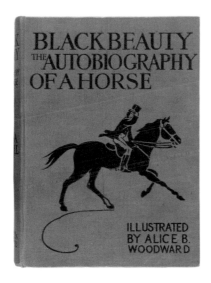

be unfinished. 'Sonia' was Sonia Graham Hodgson who played games of horses with the young princess in Hamilton Gardens. Over the course of seven chapters the story recounts the antics of Bob, Barbara, Betty and Billie and reflects the young writer's particular interest in animals. Unsurprisingly, one of Princess Elizabeth's favourite books as a child was *Black Beauty*.

Twenty or so years later, the time would come for the author of *The Happy Farm* to make the decision about where to educate her own children. Queen Elizabeth and Prince Philip chose the Buckingham Palace schoolroom as the location for Prince Charles's early learning and engaged Miss Catherine Peebles (Miss P – 'Mispy') as governess. Later however, the royal couple broke with tradition and decided that Prince Charles should attend Hill House preparatory school in Knightsbridge, and then, at the age of eight, go on to board at Cheam, where his father Prince Philip had also studied. Miss Peebles also taught Princess Anne,

ABOVE:
Princess Elizabeth's copy of *Black Beauty*, inscribed 'Elizabeth', 1931

•

BELOW:
Prince Charles returning to Cheam school, July 1958
RCIN 2814343

•

Prince Edward in the schoolroom
at Buckingham Palace alongside
his cousins Sarah Armstrong-
Jones and James Ogilvy and
governess, Lavinia Keppel, 1969
•

alongside two other little girls who joined her for lessons. Then at the age of 13 the Princess went away to school at Benenden in Kent. Her love of horses and talent for riding was further developed at the Moat House equestrian school nearby.

Prince Andrew was also taught by Miss Peebles in Buckingham Palace. However, her death in 1968, just before Prince Edward was due to start lessons, meant that, after a brief interim spell with Adele Grigg, governess to the children of Lady Susan Hussey, lady-in-waiting to The Queen, a new governess was engaged – Miss Lavinia Keppel. Prince Edward was joined in the Buckingham Palace schoolroom by a number of other children including his cousins Lady Sarah Armstrong-Jones and James Ogilvy (shown above). One schoolroom prop was a set of mathematical jigsaws which were used to teach multiplication in a fun way (opposite, top). A second room, known as the Old Schoolroom, was on the second floor and looked out over the Mall. Being larger it was used for activities such as music and movement or geography

lessons when large maps would be laid out on the floor. A piano was positioned in the corridor outside. This room was also where children's parties were often held. Both Prince Andrew and Prince Edward later went away to Heatherdown Preparatory School, near Windsor Castle and then, for their secondary education, they followed their father and their older brother, Prince Charles, to Gordonstoun in the Highlands of Scotland.

Like many children, in addition to more traditional academic subjects, royal children were also taught practical skills and attended extra-curricular classes to encourage their particular individual interests and to socialise with other children. Weekday afternoons for Princess Elizabeth and Princess Margaret during term time frequently took the form of dancing, singing or music lessons. Madame Vacani was engaged as a dancing teacher for the young princesses, and she also taught the next generation of royal children with her assistant Miss Betty, leading dancing classes in the Music Room at Buckingham Palace for Queen Elizabeth's children and their friends. In 1959 Princess Anne was given tennis lessons by Dan Maskell, while Prince Edward and Prince Andrew

LEFT:
Set of 12 mathematical jigsaw puzzles used in the schoolroom at Buckingham Palace
•
BELOW:
La Tirolienne, drawn by Princess Victoria, 12 August 1832
RCIN 980015.i
•

ABOVE LEFT:
Sketch by Princess Victoria,
Princess Royal, *c.*1850–9
RCIN 981203

●

ABOVE RIGHT:
Drawing by Prince Charles,
aged eight, 1957

●

played football. Prince Charles learnt to ice skate at Richmond Ice Rink and in March 1962, received a Certificate of Merit, Preliminary Class Standard.

As a child Princess Victoria had been taught to draw and paint by a number of artists including Richard Westall and Edwin Landseer, and spent much of her time drawing and painting. The watercolour on page 65 by Princess Victoria was painted in 1832 when she was 13 years old. It shows the ballet dancers Marie Taglioni, her brother, Paul, and his wife, Amalie Galster-Taglioni, dancing a *pas de trois* from the ballet *La Tyrolienne*. Princess Victoria delighted in going to the ballet, opera and theatre, and often sketched characters during a performance which she then later worked up into paintings in her sketchbooks at home. Queen Victoria's eldest daughter Princess Victoria inherited her mother's artistic talent and a sketch by her can be seen above left. Following in their footsteps, Prince Charles was an enthusiastic young artist – one of the prince's early works can be seen above right.

Anne Hopkins, *Sea Sense,
A Handbook on Sea
Rangering*, 1938

Queen Elizabeth enjoyed being a Girl Guide, and subsequently joined the Sea Rangers. When her daughter, Princess Anne, reached the age of eight the 1st Buckingham Palace Brownie Pack was formed, holding its weekly meetings in the gardens at Buckingham Palace, or during wet weather in the Old Schoolroom. It included children from the nearby pack at Holy Trinity, Brompton as well as the children of members of staff at the Palace. Prince Andrew and Prince Edward also attended a cub scout group at Buckingham Palace (shown overleaf).

ABOVE LEFT:
Princess Elizabeth in her
Girl Guides uniform, *c.*1942
RCIN 2002453
•

ABOVE RIGHT:
Princess Elizabeth (second from
right) with the Sea Rangers, *c.*1946
•

BELOW:
Elizabeth's Sea Ranger uniform,
*c.*1946

LEFT:
Princess Elizabeth's Girl Guide badges
*c.*1942

•

BELOW LEFT:
1st Buckingham Palace Brownie Pack,
showing Princess Anne centre top in
Buckingham Palace Garden, 1959
RCIN 2014245

•

BELOW RIGHT:
Wolf cub pack meeting, showing
Prince Andrew on the far left,
Buckingham Palace, *c.*1968
RCIN 300079

•

Tulip in a pot sewn by
Princess Elizabeth
aged 6, 1932

Fabric alphabet
book belonging
to Prince Charles,
c.1950

Blue glazed bowl
made by Prince Harry
aged 11 at Ludgrove
School

Prince William's
exercise book
1987

Princess Beatrice's
school hat, c.1992

Princess Beatrice's
riding hat, c.1993

Princesses Beatrice
and Eugenie in riding dress
at Balmoral, c.1993

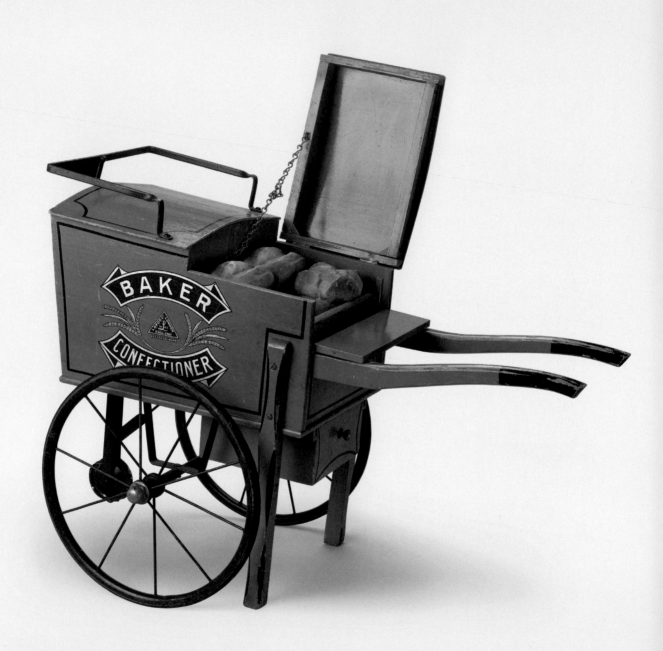

PLAYING

Playing is an essential component of life for all young children, whether royal or not. It teaches them about the world and their own place in it and allows them to develop skills such as problem solving while also promoting creativity and independence.

Behind Princess Elizabeth's home at 145 Piccadilly was a shared enclosed space, Hamilton Gardens, which provided a secure area for the young children to play outside with their parents, nanny and governess, and also provided access to Hyde Park. Security and privacy concerns naturally limit the ability for royal children to play outside in public spaces, but The Queen's children frequently played in the garden at Buckingham Palace. An area near the summer house included a sandpit and climbing frame, as well as a miniature caravan (see page 113). Princess Elizabeth also enjoyed playing on a climbing frame kept at Royal Lodge, as did Prince William at Highgrove.

Royal children played with many of the same types of toys as other children – dolls, jigsaws and train sets as well as miniature versions of adult objects like prams and wheelbarrows. As in many families, toys used by royal children were frequently passed on from one child to the next as they were outgrown and also reused by subsequent generations. One small

OPPOSITE:
Miniature baker's wagon belonging to Princess Elizabeth, c.1930

•

BELOW LEFT:
Princess Margaret in the garden of 145 Piccadilly, 1932
RCIN 2112100

•

BELOW RIGHT:
Princess Elizabeth and Princess Margaret on the climbing frame at Royal Lodge, c.1936
RCIN 2944905

•

LEFT:
Princess Elizabeth, Princess
Margaret and corgi, 1940
•

RIGHT:
Princess Anne and Prince
Charles with Queen Elizabeth,
The Queen Mother, *c.*1953
RCIN 2814310
•

BELOW:
Toy wheelbarrow with
sides shaped like a dog
RCIN 103389
•

wooden wheelbarrow in the distinctive shape of a dog still survives and appears
in a photograph of Princess Margaret, and then again being pushed by her niece
Princess Anne. Toy soldiers which had belonged to Prince Edward as a child
have been a favourite of his son, James, Viscount Severn (shown opposite).

Even before she became proficient at riding, Princess Elizabeth had a
particular love of toy horses. In the house at 145 Piccadilly a large number of
such horses on wheels were 'stabled' on the upper staircase landing beneath
a domed skylight. Each had its own saddle and bridle and they were fed and
watered every night. When the family moved to Buckingham Palace the toy
horses came too, and they occupied a new position along a corridor outside the
children's bedrooms on the second floor. Playing a game of imaginary
horses was another favourite pastime – in the photograph on
page 74 Princess Elizabeth plays a horse pulling a cart
containing Princess Margaret. The cart still survives and
demonstrates the simple construction of many of these

ABOVE LEFT:
Princess Elizabeth and Princess
Margaret with their toy horses,
*c.*1934

•

ABOVE RIGHT:
Prince Richard of Gloucester
playing with toy soldiers, *c.*1950

•

ABOVE:
Procession of toy horses
and dogs on wheels, *c.*1930
RCIN 98510–12, 98515, 98595, 98591

•

LEFT:
'The Life Guards Mounted',
toy soldiers belonging to
Prince Edward, *c.*1960

•

TOP LEFT:
Roller coaster cart
RCIN 98165

•

BOTTOM LEFT:
Miniature wooden gardening cart
RCIN 98596

TOP RIGHT:
Prince William of Gloucester
playing in the rollercoaster, *c.*1943
•

BOTTOM RIGHT:
Princess Elizabeth, Princess
Margaret and Margaret Elphinstone
playing 'horse and cart', *c.*1935
•

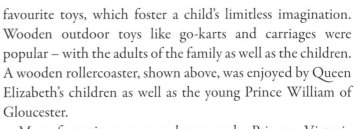

favourite toys, which foster a child's limitless imagination. Wooden outdoor toys like go-karts and carriages were popular – with the adults of the family as well as the children. A wooden rollercoaster, shown above, was enjoyed by Queen Elizabeth's children as well as the young Prince William of Gloucester.

Many favourite toys were home-made. Princess Victoria collected over 130 small wooden dolls, many of which she made with the help of her governess, Baroness Louise Lehzen. Each was individualised, some representing real people from history or contemporary society and others imaginary or drawn from the ballet or opera. 'Sir William Arnold' forms part of the fictive Arnold family, and he wears clothing made

by Princess Victoria herself – green trousers and a long overcoat (above, right). The dancer Marie Taglioni was another favourite character. She is shown, above left, dressed as 'Louise' from Michael Costa's ballet *Kenilworth* (1831). The dolls were carefully packed away by the princess once she reached her 14th birthday.

In 1938 Princess Elizabeth and Princess Margaret were presented with a pair of dolls on behalf of the children of France. The two dolls, 'France' and 'Marianne', were made by the Jumeau factory and the gift included a trousseau of over 200 items including jewellery by Cartier, clothing by Vionnet, Lanvin and Paquin, as well as lingerie, a tea set by Sèvres and a Citroën car. The gift was designed to demonstrate the extraordinary quality of French craftsmanship at the time, but was also a way of emphasising the 'entente cordiale', the strong relationship between England and France on the eve of the Second World War.

Three of Queen Victoria's home-made wooden dolls:

ABOVE LEFT:
Marie Taglioni as 'Louise' in *Kenilworth*, 1831
RCIN 72318
•

ABOVE CENTRE:
Mlle Brocard as Amy Robsart, Countess of Leicester in *Kenilworth*, 1831
RCIN 72360
•

ABOVE RIGHT:
'Sir William Arnold' 1831–3
RCIN 72387
•

ABOVE LEFT:
Princess Elizabeth and
Princess Margaret's
Poupées Raynal dolls, 1935
RCIN 107726.1–2
•

ABOVE RIGHT:
Two dolls, photographed
by Marcus Adams
on 13 December 1935
RCIN 2943725
•

Lesser known are another pair of dolls played with by the young princesses, which were made by Poupées Raynal, a Parisian doll company founded in 1922 (above left). Smaller than the Jumeau dolls, they also come with a variety of outfits by Lanvin. They appear in a set of photographs of the princesses taken by Marcus Adams in December 1935 (opposite). The dolls were deemed important enough to have a separate portrait taken – with only two human hands included to support them. Another well-loved doll belonging to Princess Elizabeth was 'Pamela', who wears a red beret and coat with plaits in her hair (overleaf, top left). In 1932 the Duchess of York purchased a Tudor

OPPOSITE:
Princess Margaret, photographed by
Marcus Adams on 13 December 1935
RCIN 2943726
•

LEFT:
Princess Elizabeth's doll 'Pamela'
wearing clothes by Smith and Co.
of Sloane Street, *c.*1935

•

RIGHT AND BELOW:
Tudor Dolls' house belonging
to Princess Elizabeth and
Princess Margaret, 1932
RCIN 21296

•

style dolls' house for her daughters at the Folkestone Exhibition of the East Kent Federation of the Women's Institutes where it had been exhibited by Miss Florence Palmer of Etchinghill, achieving full marks.

Miniature tea sets were also popular toys. A photograph taken in 1929 shows Princess Elizabeth enjoying a tea party attended by her parents and a variety of dolls while a pink 'Bunny' tea set, with which she played as a girl, is an example of the prevailing design aesthetic of 1930s toy design (above).

ABOVE:
Princess Elizabeth's
'Bunny' tea set, c.1930
•

LEFT:
The Duke and Duchess of
York with Princess Elizabeth,
photographed by Marcus Adams
on 30 July 1929
RCIN 2943782
•

ABOVE LEFT:
Princess Elizabeth's
white wickerwork
doll's pram, *c*.1928
RCIN 55918
•

ABOVE RIGHT:
Princess Elizabeth pushing her
doll's pram in Piccadilly, 1928
RCIN 2002131
•

From an early age all children naturally imitate adults, and toys that are miniature versions of adult objects allow them to copy activities going on around them. Princess Elizabeth had a wicker toy pram on wheels that she enjoyed pushing (above). Prince Edward enjoyed copying the gardeners in the grounds of Buckingham Palace with his own miniature toy lawn-mower. Prince Albert gave his children sets of gardening tools marked with their initials, and laid out rectangular beds for them in the grounds at Osborne House in which they grew their own fruit, vegetables and flowers (shown opposite).

ABOVE LEFT:
Set of gardening tools belonging
to Albert Edward (later
Edward VII)
RCIN 42999.3, 34824, 34851.1,
34872, 34825.1

•

ABOVE RIGHT:
Toy lawnmower based on the
push-lawnmowers produced by
Henry Webb in the 1950s
RCIN 98568

•

LEFT:
Children's gardening tools
at Osborne House

•

ABOVE:
Polo mallet created by Adriano 'Nano' Perez and rocking horse, made by Wilson Rocking Horses, given to Prince George of Cambridge by the President of the United States and Mrs Obama, 2013

•

OPPOSITE TOP:
Rocking horses belonging to Princess Elizabeth and Princess Margaret. They have real horse-hair manes and tails, leather bridles and saddles with blue woollen saddle cloths, c.1930–35
RCIN 100207, 100208

•

Rocking horses have been popular childhood toys since the nineteenth century. Five of Queen Victoria's grandchildren can be seen enjoying a large rocking horse built to accommodate a number of children simultaneously which is set outside the steps at Claremont (opposite, bottom left). Princesses Elizabeth and Margaret are captured in a beautifully affectionate moment on a rocking horse in a photograph by Frederick Thurston & Son, which was taken in the nursery at St Paul's Walden Bury, the country home of the Bowes Lyon family in Hertfordshire (opposite, bottom right). When their mother was a child, she had played with the same rocking horse. Each princess was also given her own very similar rocking horse, both of which were kept at Royal Lodge and positioned outside their father's office. Wearing saddles and saddle cloths emblazoned with their initials, 'C' for Caesar and 'B' for Beauty, each horse also has the Princess's initials on its bridle. A rocking horse remains a popular gift for a royal child today – Prince George received one from the President of the United States and Mrs Obama, along with a miniature polo mallet carved from an oak tree that once stood on the South Lawn of the White House (above).

LEFT:
The Duchess of Albany, wife of Prince Leopold, with Princess Alice and the Duke of Albany, Princes Alexander and Leopold and Princess Victoria Eugènie of Battenberg at Claremont House, April 1890
RCIN 204883

•

RIGHT:
Princess Elizabeth and Princess Margaret riding a rocking horse at St Paul's Walden Bury, August 1932
RCIN 2999918

•

ABOVE LEFT:
Silver filigree rattle, *c*.1762
RCIN 11944
•

ABOVE CENTRE:
Silver and coral rattle, 1774
RCIN 23129
•

ABOVE RIGHT:
Silver rattle belonging to Lady
Louise Windsor, 2003
•

Silver rattles have been a traditional toy for very young children for hundreds of years. The filigree rattle shown above left was presented to George, Prince of Wales (later George IV) in 1763 by Lady Charlotte Finch, governess to the children of George III. It was subsequently used by George III's and later by Queen Victoria's children. Another rattle used by Prince Adolphus Frederick, Duke of Cambridge, the tenth son of George III, is decorated with silver bells and set with coral, a material traditionally believed to help with the teething process (above centre). Silver rattles are still presented to newborn royal children today – a much-loved rattle belonging to Lady Louise Windsor is seen above right.

A favourite game for many young children is to build a tower of bricks and watch them come crashing down. A set of 45 alpha-numerical bricks personalised with the faces of his family was given to Prince Charles in 1949 (shown opposite) and film footage shows it being held by his mother as she encourages him to walk his first few steps at Clarence House. Another set of bricks is contained within a wooden trolley labelled 'Prince Charles Express' and is still played with by the current generation of royal children.

'Whimsey Bits' jigsaw puzzle
belonging to Princess Elizabeth,
*c.*1930

Prince Charles's trolley of
toy blocks, *c.*1950
RCIN 95167

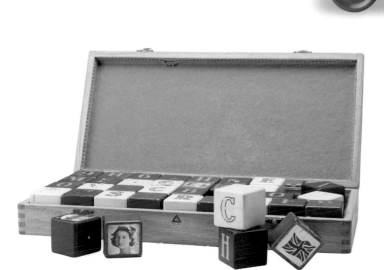

Toy building blocks given to
Prince Charles in 1949
RCIN 40876

ABOVE LEFT:
Prince William playing football
at Kensington Palace, 1984
RCIN 2115711

•

ABOVE RIGHT:
Prince William and Prince
Richard of Gloucester playing
chess, c.1950

•

RIGHT:
Prince William of Gloucester
playing with a train set, c.1947

•

'Knockemdown Ninepins' belonging
to Princess Elizabeth, c.1930
RCIN 101032

Teddy from the Royal Nursery
RCIN 98519

Noah's Ark and animals
belonging to Princess Elizabeth,
c.1930

Model train set of the Paris
Metro in a presentation case
made by Louis Vuitton
RCIN 92360

DRESSING

Decisions about the types of clothing worn by royal children have traditionally been made by royal parents and nannies. While royal parents have tended to have the final say on matters of style, practical considerations such as the purchasing, laundering, pressing and mending of the children's clothing have often fallen under the remit of the royal nanny. Historically, the royal nanny was also responsible for dressing her royal charges. So fond was Princess Elizabeth of her nursery maid Margaret MacDonald, that, on being crowned Queen in 1953, she appointed her as her official Dresser.

Today, little survives of the larger body of children's clothing once owned by the royal family. Moreover, records of dress now preserved in paintings and photographs often present only a partial view of what royal children actually wore, showing only formal or 'new' items looking at their best.

Of the items of clothing that do survive, ceremonial clothes, worn infrequently and stored carefully when no longer required, tend to be in the best condition. The page and bridesmaid outfits worn by Zara and Peter Phillips for the marriage of the Duke of York to Sarah Ferguson (shown on page 90), for example, are in very good condition. An official photograph taken in the Throne Room at Buckingham Palace on the occasion of the Duke and Duchess's wedding (shown right), shows Zara and her brother Peter (both seated, front centre) in the outfits specially commissioned for the occasion. Zara's handmade peach shoes with lace rosette detailing were made by Glanville-Sharpe.

OPPOSITE:
Princess Elizabeth and Princess Margaret on a shopping trip, 1934
RCIN 2999836
•

BELOW:
The wedding of the Duke and Duchess of York, 23 July 1986
•

ABOVE LEFT:
Bridesmaid dress and shoes worn
by Zara Phillips, 1986

•

ABOVE RIGHT:
Pageboy outfit and shoes worn by
Peter Phillips, 1986

•

Keen to detach herself from the extravagant spending associated with the Hanoverian dynasty, Queen Victoria was one of the first monarchs to take a decidedly thrifty approach to clothing, both for herself and her children. Once outgrown, items of dress were often passed down through the family and re-worn by younger children. In July 1844, Queen Victoria recorded in her journal, having attended chapel at Buckingham Palace in the morning that 'Alice came down to luncheon, in the Tyrolese costume which Vicky wore on my birthday 2 years ago.' This re-using of childhood clothing is still practised by the current royal family.

As representatives of the royal family, royal children have always been expected to dress elegantly when out in public. Formal coats were often adopted, such as the two beautiful pink coats worn by Princess Elizabeth and Princess Margaret and made by Smith & Co. of Sloane Street (shown opposite, top left). They can also be seen in a number of press photographs taken of the

LEFT:
Princess Elizabeth's and Princess Margaret's matching pink coats, made by Smith & Co., c.1934

•

RIGHT:
The Duchess of York leaving the Royal Horse Show at Olympia with Princess Elizabeth and Princess Margaret, 26 June 1934
RCIN 2108309

•

LEFT:
Prince William's blue jacket, made by the Chelsea Design Co. Ltd, c.1987

•

RIGHT:
Prince William and Princess Diana during the Trooping the Colour parade, 13 June 1987

•

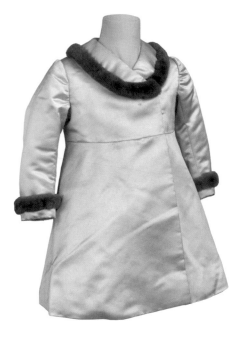

Satin coat and hat worn by Princess Margaret, made by Smith & Co., c.1934
•

Princess Margaret with Queen Mary at the wedding of the Duke of Kent to Princess Marina of Greece, 1934
•

BELOW:
Prince Andrew and Prince Edward playing in the snow at Sandringham, December 1969
•

two girls during outings with their mother. Popular with the royal family, this style of knee-length, double-breasted overcoat with a decorative or contrasting collar is often referred to as a princess coat. Formal coats were also standard for young boys when appearing in public. Prince William, for example, appeared in a pale blue coat with peaked lapels for the Trooping The Colour ceremony in 1987 (shown on the previous page). Clothing worn by young royal children in private was much more informal, as the winter coats and bobble hats worn by Prince Andrew and Prince Edward during the Christmas break at Sandringham demonstrate (left).

The Queen Mother evidently took a particular interest in dressing her children and much of what they wore reflects her personal style. A cream satin coat with fur trim and matching hat worn by Princess Margaret for the wedding of the Duke of Kent

LEFT:
White dress worn by Princess
Elizabeth, c.1930
•

RIGHT:
Dresses worn by Princess Beatrice
and Princess Eugenie, c.1988–1992
•

LEFT:
Princess Elizabeth, photographed
by Marcus Adams in 1931
RCIN 2943711
•

RIGHT:
Prince Richard of Gloucester,
c.1945
•

to Princess Marina of Greece and Denmark in 1934 (shown opposite), is typical
of the Queen Mother's love of soft furs and elegant headwear.

Despite its impracticality, garments worn by babies have historically been
white. For many years, white not only served as a symbol of purity, but also
avoided the use of coloured dyes which faded quickly with the repeated washing
children's clothing requires, and, in some cases, could be poisonous.

ABOVE LEFT:
The 'Blonde' dress worn by
Princess Victoria, *c.*1830
RCIN 74872

•

ABOVE RIGHT:
Richard Westall,
Queen Victoria when a Girl, 1830
RCIN 400135

•

The practice of dressing royal infants in white continued into the twentieth century. A number of fine, white linen dresses worn by Princess Elizabeth and Princess Margaret still survive, and are similar to examples seen in photographs by Marcus Adams (shown on page 93). Simple white frocks with coloured smocking at the chest were popular throughout the twentieth century, as seen in a photograph of Prince Richard of Gloucester. Similar white cotton dresses with simple decoration continued to be worn during the 1980s by Princess Beatrice and Princess Eugenie (page 93).

In the nineteenth century white remained a popular colour for young girls beyond infancy. A beautiful white dress is one of the earliest surviving garments known to have been worn by Queen Victoria (shown above). Constructed from a series of bobbin-lace panels made from unbleached silk rather than

linen, the dress is often referred to as the 'Blonde dress' owing to its luxurious and shimmering, glossy appearance. It is likely that this dress was presented to Queen Victoria as a gift by her uncle Leopold, King of the Belgians, and his French wife Louise-Marie. As Queen Adelaide had put a ban on the wearing of foreign textiles in her Dressing Room, the dress was probably never worn on a state occasion.

Until the early twentieth century, both boys and girls would have worn skirts or short dresses in their infancy. Painted by Johan Zoffany shortly after George III and his family moved into Buckingham House, the painting on page 6 shows the King's two eldest sons in the type of loose-fitting, silk coats and wide sashes worn by young boys in the mid-eighteenth century.

ABOVE LEFT:
Blue velvet jacket with applied lace, 1868
RCIN 71965.a
•

ABOVE RIGHT:
Red velvet walking suit with miniver trim, c.1867–8
RCIN 71941.a-b
•

Princess Elizabeth and
Princess Margaret at Windsor Castle,
photographed by Studio Lisa, *c*.1940
RCIN 2002156

Walking suits, with skirts rather than trousers, were popular for slightly older boys during the nineteenth century. A blue velvet walking suit, trimmed with white lace, and a red velvet example, trimmed with white fur, were both worn by Prince George (later King George V). Such suits were often made in matching pairs – a larger red velvet suit was made for Prince George's elder brother, Albert Victor. This tradition of dressing royal siblings alike continued into the twentieth century when Princess Elizabeth and Princess Margaret were frequently photographed in identical outfits. A photograph taken at Windsor Castle in 1941 shows the two princesses dressed in matching patterned dresses with laced-edged collars and plain leather shoes.

Another characteristic of the young princesses day dresses is their loose fit. Historically, royal children have not always been allowed to dress so comfortably. During the sixteenth and seventeenth centuries the clothing worn by children tended to be structured and restrictive, often giving the impression of children dressed as miniature adults. By contrast, the children of George III grew up in a period marked by a distinctive change in attitude towards childhood and,

accordingly, children's dress. The new style that emerged in the mid-eighteenth century allowed for greater freedom of movement and accommodated children's natural development. In Singleton Copley's portrait of *The Three Youngest Daughters of George III* (shown on page 10), two-year old Princess Amelia, seated in the carriage, wears a loosely fitting white cotton frock with a wide blue sash. Lighter fabrics and higher waistbands have replaced the stiffened bodices fashionable 50 years earlier.

Similarly, for young boys, a new form of dress, designed specifically for children, appeared in the 1780s and was known as the skeleton suit. The portrait above left, painted by the American artist Benjamin West in 1783, depicts George III's eighth son Prince Octavius wearing a golden-yellow skeleton suit with an open frilled-collared shirt. The skeleton suit was designed to be worn as a complete ensemble; it consisted of a

ABOVE LEFT:
Benjamin West, *Prince Octavius*, 1783
RCIN 401410
•

ABOVE CENTRE:
Sir Joshua Reynolds, *John Charles ('Jack'), later the 3rd Earl Spencer*, 1786
•

ABOVE RIGHT:
Prince Harry with Lady Sarah McCorquodale at the wedding of Viscount Althorp to Victoria Lockwood, 17 September 1989
•

RIGHT:
Pageboy outfit worn by Prince Harry, 1989
•

ABOVE LEFT:
Franz Xaver Winterhalter, *Albert Edward, Prince of Wales*, 1846
RCIN 404873

•

ABOVE RIGHT:
Princes Edward, Albert and Henry of Wales and Princess Mary of Wales, 1902
RCIN 2144478

•

pair of high-waisted, front-fastening trousers buttoned into a fitted jacket. The cream silk outfit worn in 1989 by Prince Harry as a five-year-old pageboy at the wedding of his uncle, Viscount Althorp, to Victoria Lockwood is reminiscent of this style of clothing and was inspired by a portrait of John Charles Spencer by Sir Joshua Reynolds, which dates from 1786 and hangs in the Spencer family home at Althorp (both shown on page 97).

The royal family have, on occasion, found themselves not simply adopting the styles of the day (as with the skeleton suit), but also setting the trend for

popular children's wear. In 1846, shortly before the family departed on a visit to the Channel Islands, Queen Victoria ordered a child-sized sailor suit for the young Prince of Wales which she purchased from a British naval outfitting supplier and was modelled on the uniforms worn by regular sailors in the Royal Navy. In December of the same year, Prince Albert presented his wife with, in her own words, a 'lovely full length picture of Bertie, in his sailor dress, by Winterhalter' (opposite, top left). Liberally reproduced and widely circulated in the form of engravings, Winterhalter's portrait soon sparked a fashion for sailor suits that would survive well into the twentieth century. A photograph taken in 1902 shows the future Kings Edward VIII and George VI in matching nautical outfits alongside their younger sister, Mary, and brother Henry, later Duke of Gloucester (opposite, top right). In 1986 Prince William wore a child-sized sailor suit, complete with matching straw boater, at the wedding of his uncle, The Duke of York (above).

ABOVE LEFT:
Prince William dressed in his pageboy outfit at the wedding of The Duke and Duchess of York, 23 July 1986
•

ABOVE RIGHT:
Prince William's sailor suit for the wedding of the Duke and Duchess of York, 1986
•

ABOVE LEFT:
Waistcoat, kilt and sporran made
for Albert Edward, Prince of
Wales (later Edward VII), *c*.1844

•

ABOVE RIGHT:
Sir William Ross, *Albert Edward,
Prince of Wales and
Prince Alfred*, 1847
RCIN 913818

•

Another style made popular by Queen Victoria and her family was Highland dress inspired by her love of Scotland. A child-sized kilt, waistcoat and sporran were purchased by the Queen, from Meyer and Mortimer, for her eldest son Albert Edward. The future king appears to be wearing the same sporran and a

similar kilt in a watercolour by Sir William Ross, painted for the Queen in 1847 (shown opposite). Albert Edward's younger brother, Alfred, is shown wearing a full sporran, made from the complete pelt of what appears to be a pine marten.

This fashion for Highland dress continued into the following century with commercially made 'Scottish suits' starting to be stocked in small shops and department stores. In 1958, Prince Charles and Princess Anne were photographed wearing kilts at the Braemar Games in Aberdeenshire. The labels on the surviving kilts tell us that some of these items were altered – either enlarged as the children got older, or passed down through the family and reduced in size where necessary. Tartan remains a popular fabric for royal children in the twenty-first century. Lady Louise Windsor wore a tartan dress (above left) at the age of one in a formal photograph taken at Balmoral with her parents and grandparents.

ABOVE LEFT:
Tartan dress worn by Lady Louise Windsor, c.2004
•

ABOVE CENTRE:
Prince Charles's tweed jacket, kilt and sporran as worn for the Braemar Games, 1958
•

ABOVE RIGHT:
The Royal Family at the Braemar Games, Aberdeenshire, 1958
•

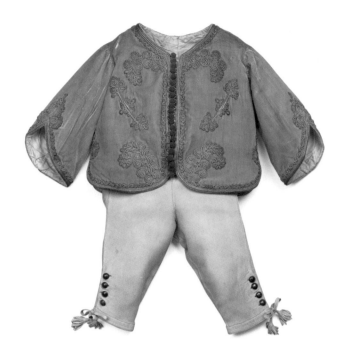

ABOVE LEFT:
Prince Alfred as 'Autumn',
Tableaux of the Seasons series,
photographed by Roger Fenton,
May 1854
RCIN 2943820

•

ABOVE RIGHT:
Blue velvet jacket with gold
embroidery and buckskin
breeches worn by Albert Edward,
Prince of Wales, c.1845–7

•

Dressing up and creative play have always been important to children in the royal nursery. Queen Victoria was particularly fond of the theatre and the royal children were often arranged into tableaux by their tutors and governesses, to be presented as a surprise for their parents.

On 10 February, 1854, and to celebrate the fourteenth wedding anniversary of Queen Victoria and Prince Albert, the children performed one of their most ambitious tableaux to date. Staged in the Rubens Room at Windsor Castle, the elder children appeared dressed as the Four Seasons; Alice as Spring, Vicky as Summer, Alfred as Bacchus, representing Autumn (above, left), and Albert Edward as Winter, dressed as an old man with a long white beard. A

Princess Elizabeth, Princess Margaret and Hubert Tannar dressed for a performance of *Cinderella*, 1941
RCIN 2089820

blue, Turkish-style jacket with buckskin breeches is believed to have been worn by Albert Edward, when Prince of Wales, during another of these familial performances.

George III commissioned a number of portraits of both himself, and his family, in clothing that departed from eighteenth century fashionable styles; a form of fancy dress for portraiture. This style, known as 'Vandyke dress', was based on the types of clothing popular in the 1630s and portrayed in paintings by Sir Anthony van Dyck. In the delicate porcelain grouping shown on page 9, modelled after a contemporary portrait by Johan Zoffany, the three eldest sons of George III are dressed in this style of historical costume. The future George IV, shown at the centre of the left-hand grouping, for example, wears an elaborate lace collar and doublet complete with seventeenth-century slashing.

During the Second World War, the royal family staged a series of pantomimes in the Waterloo Chamber at Windsor Castle. The plays were devised and scripted by the two royal princesses with the guidance of Hubert Tannar, Headmaster at the Royal School in Windsor Great Park, and the money raised through ticket sales was donated to their mother's wartime wool fund. The first pantomime, *Cinderella* was performed in 1941. In one photograph taken during a rehearsal, Princess Elizabeth appears dressed as the dashing Prince Florizel and Princess Margaret as Cinderella (previous page). Tannar sometimes also starred in the pantomimes alongside the princesses, and most of the costumes were made by the Castle seamstress, making use of discarded dresses and furnishing fabrics.

Royal birthday parties also provided occasions for dressing up. A series of photographs, taken by Leonida Caldesi in April 1859, record the royal children dressed in the costumes worn for the 'Fancy Ball' in celebration of Prince Leopold's sixth birthday. The two princesses, Helena and Louise, wear traditional Swiss costume, while their younger brother appears dressed as a son

LEFT:
Princess Helena and Princess Louise in traditional Swiss costume, 7 April 1859
RCIN 2900163
•

RIGHT:
Prince Leopold dressed as a son of Henry IV for his sixth birthday party, 7 April 1859
RCIN 2900167
•

ABOVE LEFT:
Fairy doll belonging
to Princess Anne
RCIN 98579

•

ABOVE RIGHT:
Fairy costume, wand and tiara
worn by Princess Anne

•

LEFT:
Princess Anne and Prince Charles
in fancy dress for Prince Charles's
fifth birthday party, 1953
RCIN 210254

•

LEFT:
Green shorts and white shirt
worn by Prince Harry, *c.*1988

•

RIGHT:
Diana, Princess of Wales
and young Prince Harry at
Buckingham Palace for Trooping
the Colour, 1 June 1988

•

LEFT:
Blue shorts and white shirt worn
by Prince William, *c.*1985

•

RIGHT:
Prince Charles with Prince
William on the Royal Yacht
Britannia on May 6, 1985

•

of Henry IV (shown on page 104 bottom right). The four children can also be seen dressed in their fancy dress costumes in the watercolour by Eugenio Agneni, reproduced on page 29.

In 1953, Queen Elizabeth II hosted a similar, fancy dress party at Buckingham Palace to celebrate Prince Charles's fifth birthday. On this occasion Princess Anne wore a tiny fairy costume complete with wings, tiara and magic wand while photographs taken at the time show the young Prince dressed as Robin Hood, carrying a bow and arrows (shown on page 105). A similar fairy costume worn by Princess Anne several years later also survives along with a doll dressed in an identical outfit.

Military dress also influenced more casual styles of royal clothing. This soldier dressing gown belonged to Prince Harry and was worn by the young prince when he underwent an operation at the age of three at Great Ormond Street hospital, *c.*1987

•

GETTING AROUND

In 1846, the Dowager Queen Adelaide, widow of King William IV, presented her grandchildren with one of the first of many small-scale vehicles to be given to the royal children over the next 150 years. The child-sized, donkey-drawn barouche (shown below), complete with claret-coloured interior, folding hood, C-scroll suspension springs (for extra comfort) and a raised seat for a young driver, was made to look almost identical in style to the one used by Queen Victoria and Prince Albert. A photograph, taken outside Osborne House in 1884, shows three of Queen Victoria's grandchildren seated in the carriage: Princess Margaret and Prince Arthur, the two eldest children of Arthur, Duke of Connaught, and their cousin, Princess Alice of Albany (opposite). In January 1884, Queen Victoria sent this photograph, alongside a letter, to Prince George of Wales, in which she describes the carriage as being drawn by, 'the little white donkey I have had since a foal & it used to run about in the Windsor Home Park fields.'

Pulled by horses but on a slightly smaller scale, the royal children also owned a number of miniature wooden horse-drawn carriages. In a photograph taken in 1899 outside York Cottage on the Sandringham Estate, Prince Albert, later George VI and his elder brother Prince Edward, later Edward VIII, are shown playing with a beautiful, pedal-powered carriage complete with two white horses and a wicker driving chair (shown overleaf). Another slightly less ornate pedal-powered carriage was used by a young Prince Charles (overleaf). Like the earlier

OPPOSITE:
Three of Queen Victoria's grandchildren in the miniature barouche presented by Queen Adelaide, January 1884
RCIN 2904041

•

BELOW:
Miniature barouche *c*.1840, built by Corbens of Twickenham and housed in the Royal Mews, Buckingham Palace

•

ABOVE LEFT:
Prince Charles playing on a
pedal-powered horse and cart
RCIN 2814282

•

ABOVE RIGHT:
Prince Edward and Prince Albert of
York (later King Edward VIII and King
George VI), outside York Cottage,
May 1897
RCIN 2373313

•

example, a pedal mechanism, attached to the back wheels, is used to power the carriage and a set of red reins, attached to both the front wheel and the horse's bridle, is used by way of steering.

With the emergence of motor cars at the end of the nineteenth century, both car manufacturers and toy makers soon turned their attention to miniature reproductions. An electric Citroën, produced in the late 1920s and given to the Princesses Elizabeth and Margaret, was certainly at the top of the range. The car, originally made by André Citroën as a gift for his son Miki in 1928, was modelled on the full-size C4. Only a small number were produced, making this model extremely rare. A photograph shows George VI crouching behind the car while Princess Elizabeth sits giggling in the driving seat (opposite, bottom left). The car was renovated for Prince Charles in 1953, at which stage the original Citroën radiator was replaced by a new Daimler

LEFT:
Pedal-powered horse and cart
used by Prince Charles
RCIN 98558

•

design, and the registration number was appropriately changed to PC 1953.

In addition to inheriting his mother's Citroën, Prince Charles also had his own, much-loved pedal car. Produced by Britain's leading toy manufacturer, Tri-ang, this model, known as the Centurion, was one of the company's most ambitious creations (above right). Advertised as 'the finest equipped pedal motor in the world', the little green car came complete with electric head lamps and tail lights, cushion-tired wheels with chrome caps, working boot, handbrake and a dash-board mounted radio. The Prince can be seen sitting in the car in a photograph taken outside Balmoral (below, right). This pedal car is still used by the current generation of royal children.

ABOVE LEFT:
Toy Citroën belonging to
Princess Elizabeth and Princess
Margaret, c.1928
RCIN 38650

•

ABOVE RIGHT:
Tri-ang Centurion
model car first used by
Prince Charles, c.1950
RCIN 21589

•

LEFT:
George VI with his daughters
Princess Elizabeth and
Princess Margaret outside
Royal Lodge, 1934
RCIN 2112476

•

RIGHT:
Queen Elizabeth II and
Prince Charles at Balmoral,
photographed by Studio Lisa,
28 September 1952
RCIN 2584996

•

LEFT:
Tri-ang orange tractor
and trailer, *c.*1950
RCIN 103396

•

RIGHT:
Tri-ang tractor, *c.*1950
RCIN 92288

•

BELOW:
Miniature Aston Martin presented
to Prince Andrew in 1966
RCIN 38637

•

Fond of the outdoors and farming even as a child, Prince Charles also had a series of child-sized farming vehicles. A three-wheeled toy tractor, also produced by Tri-ang and known as 'Major', came with a trailer so that the young Prince could accommodate a passenger.

Of all the royal children, it is Prince Andrew who must have been most envied by his friends when, at the age of just six, he was presented, by Aston Martin, with a miniature replica of the DB5 used by James Bond in the films *Goldfinger* and *Thunderball*. Not only was the car fully mobile with a top speed of ten miles per hour, it had all the gadgets famously added to the full-size vehicle in the films; rotating number plates, extendable over-riders, a pop-up bullet proof shield, machine guns concealed behind

D.M. Linder of Rollalong,
designer of the royal caravan
with Diana Gordon Bennett,
interior designer, 1955
•

the side lights, a working smoke screen and electric water jets hidden in the rear reflectors.

In 1955, the British Caravan Club presented the young Prince Charles and Princess Anne with one of their most unusual toys; a specially designed miniature Rollalong caravan (above). At less than seven feet long, the caravan came with its own water, gas and electricity supply, child-sized kitchen, miniature tea set (shown overleaf) and complete collection of Beatrix Potter books. As it was not motorised, the caravan was fitted with a tow-hitch enabling the Duke of

ABOVE:
Poole Pottery tea service from
The Royal Caravan, *c.*1955
•

BELOW:
Red tricycle first used by
Princess Anne, *c.*1953
RCIN 250696
•

Edinburgh to pull the children around the grounds of Buckingham Palace in an old Hillman Husky, borrowed from the Royal Mews. The caravan was kept in the garden at Buckingham Palace near the sandpit and climbing frame, and was often played with by The Queen's children. In 1982, the caravan was refurbished and re-presented to Princess Anne. It was later completely restored by the original builders, Rollalong, on the occasion of the club's centenary in 2007.

In addition to these unique and rather luxurious children's vehicles usually presented by their makers, the royal children also enjoyed playing with the same kind of tricycles that many people might recognise from their own childhood. In a photograph taken in 1931, Princess Elizabeth is shown riding through the park on her tricycle with a pram, containing her sister Margaret, being pushed behind her (opposite, top left). Twenty years later, The Queen and the young Princess Anne, were similarly recorded enjoying a summer ride on two shiny, red tricycles. This pair of tricycles are still used by the royal children today.

ABOVE LEFT:
Princess Elizabeth riding
her tricycle, 1931
RCIN 2002135
•

ABOVE RIGHT:
Princess Elizabeth and Princess
Margaret photographed by
Studio Lisa, 1940
RCIN 2002167
•

In 2013, this tradition continued when Boris Johnson, Mayor of London, presented Prince George with a tricycle, modelled on the London 'Boris Bikes'. This gift both marked the occasion of the Prince's birth and was, in the Mayor's own words, intended to 'acculturate him to the joy of cycling' at the earliest opportunity (left). The tricycle is fitted so that it can be attached to the 'Boris-style' tandem presented to the Duke and Duchess as a wedding present in 2011, and the serial number reads 220713, the prince's date of birth.

LEFT:
Blue tricycle given to
Prince George by Boris Johnson,
Mayor of London, in 2013
•

PICTURE CREDITS

Page 1   A selection of shoes worn by royal children during the nineteenth and early twentieth century, RCIN 72253, 72252, 71937 and Museum of London

Page 2   Princess Elizabeth with two corgis at her home at 145 Piccadilly, photographed by Studio Lisa, July 1936, RCIN 2305569

Page 3   Procession of toy horses and dogs on wheels, c.1930, RCIN 98510–12, 98515, 98595, 98591

Page 4   'Knockemdown Ninepins' belonging to Princess Elizabeth, c.1930, RCIN 101032

Page 119 Princess Elizabeth and Princess Margaret playing in the sand at St Paul's Walden Bury, Hertfordshire, 1933, RCIN 2112259

Page 120 Doll dressed in a sailor outfit, belonging to Princess Elizabeth, c.1935, RCIN 250695

Unless otherwise stated, all images are Royal Collection Trust/© Her Majesty Queen Elizabeth II 2014

Royal Collection Trust is grateful for permission to reproduce the following:

© Museum of London, pp. 1, 22, 100
Studio Lisa © Getty Images, pp. 2, 96, 103, 115
Kensington Palace, Historic Royal Palaces, p. 11
The Royal Archives, p. 12 RA VIC/MAIN/Z/262/1846/71; p. 41 RA QEQM/PRIV/CHILD, p. 59 RA VIC/ADDA7/1A/4, RA GV/PRIV/AA2, p. 60 RA QM/PRIV/CC10/2, RA QM/PRIV/CC10/8
Royal Collection Trust/All Rights Reserved, pp. 14, 18, 25, 49, 61, 67, 69, 71, 73, 74, 86, 91, 92, 93, 110, 111
Photograph by Snowdon/Trunk Archive ©Armstrong Jones pp. 17, 26-7, 52
© Press Association Images, pp. 20, 21, 29, 35, 36, 51, 53, 89, 91, 97, 99, 106
© Newangle Creative Agency, p. 24
Archive of Her Majesty's Chapel Royal, St James's Palace © Her Majesty Queen Elizabeth II, p. 33
© Joan Williams, pp. 64, 92
© Getty Images, p. 72
Topical Press Agency Ltd./All Rights Reserved, pp. 80, 88
© English Heritage, p. 81
Frederick Thursten & Son/All Rights Reserved, p. 83
© Althorp, p. 97
Photograph by Camera Press London, p. 101
Wallace Heaton Ltd./All Rights Reserved, p. 105
© The Caravan Club Collection, p. 113
© Keystone Press Agency, p. 115

ACKNOWLEDGEMENTS

The authors would like to acknowledge the support and gracious permission of Her Majesty The Queen for the undertaking of the exhibition at Buckingham Palace and the publication of this book, and the generous co-operation of the many members of The Royal Family who have contributed precious possessions and memories.

Further thanks for help in numerous practical ways are due to Mabel Anderson, Lady Susan Hussey, Sandra Bull, Angela Kelly, Virginia Carington, Leslie Chappell, Debbie Fawcett, Nick Wright, Amanda Thirsk, Suzanne Lofthouse-Jackson, Annabelle Galletley, Alastair Todd, Nicholas Marden, Rebecca Deacon, Helen Asprey, Gemma Kaza and Tyne Gibson. We would also like to thank Geoffrey Weiner for his expert opinion on miniature pedal cars, and Joan Williams for sharing her experience of photographing the royal family during the 1960s. Our thanks also go out to Historic Royal Palaces, the Museum of London and the National Motor Museum, Beaulieu, who have all loaned items to this exhibition and have allowed us to reproduce their images in this book.

For their help with research and in many other aspects of the project we would like to acknowledge the assistance of Royal Collection Trust colleagues Sandra Adler, Stephen Chapman, Louise Cooling, Sally Goodsir, Caroline de Guitaut, Lisa Heighway, Kathryn Jones, Jill Kelsey, Karen Lawson, Jonathan Marsden, Alessandro Nasini, Daniel Partridge, Lauren Porter, Tim Ritson, Sabrina Stevenson, Shaun Turner, Tung Tsin Lam, Jane Wallis, David Wheeler and Eva Zielinska-Millar. For their help in preparing the clothing and measuring for the many mannequins required for both the exhibition and publication, we would like to thank Deborah Phipps and Ashley Backhouse. Finally, we would like to thank the publishing team, in particular Elizabeth Simpson, Paul Sloman and Debbie Wayment, for all their hard work and long hours in putting this book together.

To find out more about the Royal Collection please visit our website www.royalcollection.org.uk
Subscribe to Royal Collection Trust's e-newsletter at www.royalcollection.org.uk/newsletter

Written by Anna Reynolds and Lucy Peter

Published by Royal Collection Trust
York House
St James's Palace
London SW1A 1BQ

Royal Collection Trust / © Her Majesty Queen Elizabeth II 2014

All rights reserved. Except as permitted under legislation, no part of this work may be photocopied,
stored in a retrieval system, published, performed in public, adapted, broadcast, transmitted, recorded
or reproduced in any form or by any means, without the prior permission of the copyright owner.

ISBN 978 1 909741 11 9

014913

British Library Cataloguing in Publication Data:
A catalogue record of this book is available from the British Library.

Designed by +SUBTRACT
Production Manager Debbie Wayment
Project Manager Elizabeth Simpson
Colour reproduction by Altaimage London
Printed on Gardmat 150gsm
Printed and bound in Slovenia by Gorenjski tisk

To find out more about the Royal Collection
please visit our website www.royalcollection.org.uk